STD

FRIENDS
OF ACPL

3 1833 00649 8353

D1269272

The FIRST BOOK of PUERTO RICO

El Yunque Rain Forest

The FIRST BOOK of
PUERTO RICO

by ANTONIO J. COLORADO

Illustrated with photographs

FRANKLIN WATTS, INC.
575 Lexington Ave., New York 10022

Photographs courtesy of:

Author, page 32
Carl Levin Assoc. Inc., pages 34, 37, 42, 43, 45, 49, 50, 52, 55, 57 bottom,
  64
F. Colorado, page 21
Commonwealth of Puerto Rico, half title, pages 15, 16, 23,
  24, 26, 27, 28, 29, 44, 53, 54, 56, 57 top, 67
Economic Development Administration, cover, title page left, pages 12, 13,
  39, 40, 59, 62 top, 68
Pan-American Coffee Bureau, page 10
Puerto Rico Dept. of Agriculture, pages 4, 5, 6, 7, 8, 9, 14, 18, 30, 31,
  62 bottom, 65, 66
Puerto Rico News Service, page 38
U. S. Navy photograph, opp. page 1
R. Velez, University of Puerto Rico, pages 46, 47

JACKET PHOTO Luquillo Beach, Puerto Rico

© Copyright 1965 by Franklin Watts, Inc.
Library of Congress Catalog Card Number: 65-11743
Printed in the United States of America by
Polygraphic Company of America
4   5

CONTENTS

1422812

Hurricane Hunter

THE LAND

In the Path of the Evil God

EVERY DAY, beginning on the morning of each June fifteenth and continuing through September, powerful Hurricane Hunters leave the Roosevelt Roads United States Naval Station in Puerto Rico (PWAIR-toe REE-ko) to hunt for hurricanes. When they find one they follow its every move, fly into its eye, and inform the citizens of Puerto Rico and the neighboring islands of its course. This advance warning keeps the loss of life due to hurricanes to a minimum.

But it wasn't always like this. The *Borinquén* (bo-reen-KANE) Indians of Puerto Rico once feared the evil hurricane god *Juracán* even more than they feared the cannibalistic Caribs. Sometimes they could win a battle with the Caribs but they always lost when Juracán came roaring across their island.

The Borinquens may have wondered why "The Evil God" should visit them so often. Today we know it is simply because the island of Puerto Rico is in a hurricane zone. These tropical storms that attack Puerto Rico begin in the Atlantic Ocean between Africa and the West Indies.

1

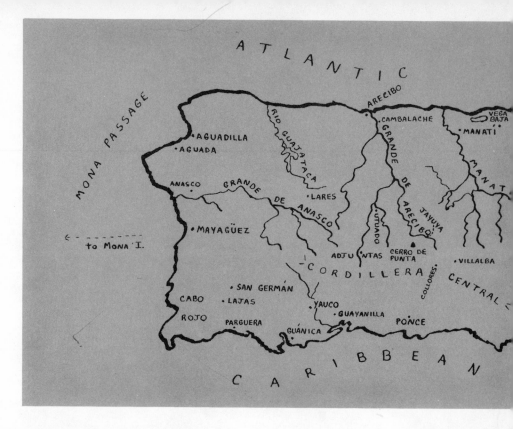

Location, Mountains, Climate

PUERTO RICO, which looks like a rough rectangle, is the smallest and most easterly of the Greater Antilles, a group of four islands in the West Indies. Roughly one hundred miles long and thirty-five miles wide, it is pounded by the Atlantic Ocean on the north and lapped by the Caribbean Sea on the south. Several smaller islands are also considered part of Puerto Rico. The three largest of these are the uninhabited island of Mona to the west, and Vieques (vee-AY-kayce) and Culebra (koo-LAY-brah) off the east coast.

The greatest air travel center in the Caribbean, Puerto Rico is 1,600 miles from New York; 1,050 miles from Miami, Florida; 4,000 miles from Madrid, Spain; and 550 miles from Caracas, Venezuela.

The island of Puerto Rico is really the top of a large submerged mountain chain which extends southeastward from off the coast of Florida

2

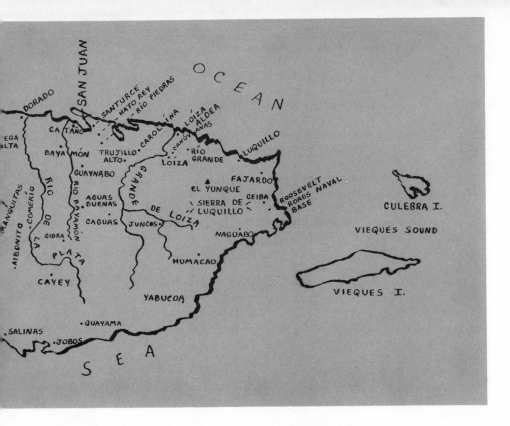

almost to Venezuela. The waters around Puerto Rico are very deep. In fact, about forty-five miles to the northwest is one of the deepest spots in the world— 30,246 feet from the surface of the Atlantic to the ocean floor. If all the waters around the island were to dry up, Puerto Rico, sitting on top of this mountain range, would be higher than the highest mountain in the world, Mt. Everest, at 29,028 feet!

Even though the island is small, it can be divided into four different sections: the northern and eastern coasts, with their constant trade winds and heavy rainfall; the central mountain ranges and hills (the Cordillera Central and the Luquillo Range); the dry southern country where irrigation is necessary for an efficient production of crops; and the triangular western coastal valleys, wet in summer and dry in winter.

Puerto Rico's temperature changes very little from summer to winter. The official average is 76 degrees Fahrenheit, but it often reaches 90 degrees on the coasts, especially during midday. The hottest months of

3

Flowers grow everywhere.

the year are August, September, and October. However, as soon as you drive into the mountains, half an hour from the capital city of San Juan (sahn WHAHN), the temperature drops as much as ten degrees.

Plant Life

THE PUERTO RICAN countryside is green and flowering all through the year. Still, only a relatively small part of the land is good for commercial agriculture, due to erosion, forest clearing, and misuse in the past.

Puerto Ricans love nature. Even the city dwellers have a love for growing things that no amount of sidewalks and skyscrapers can erase. Flowers and plants grow as if by magic. In fact, it's not unusual for fence cuttings to sprout branches and leaves!

All the usual tropical flowers grow in Puerto Rico — hibiscus, poinsettias, gardenias, heliotropes, and many others. Most interesting, however, are the wild flowers with their picturesque names, such as *lágrimas de pobre* (tears of the poor); *rabo de ratón* (rattail); *bandera española* (Spanish flag); and *morí-viví* (it dies, it lives). The morí-viví is a fascinating plant because its leaves completely close up when they touch a strange object. When the object is removed, the leaves slowly open again. However, if you visit Puerto Rico, you should be careful of the morí-viví (everybody wants to touch it to see it die and live again) because its ground-crawling stem contains hundreds of almost invisible thorns.

4

Wild orchids

Most of Puerto Rico's wild flowers are tiny. Many are no larger than a baby's fingernail. Each one is a beautiful floral miniature, just as Puerto Rico is a beautiful country in miniature.

You don't have to travel to the Rain Forest in the Luquillo Range to see tiny wild orchids. Anyone with sharp eyes can see these and other epiphytes (plants which grow harmlessly on other plants) clinging to trees or rocks along the roads leading to the mountains.

Hardwood and softwood trees grow in Puerto Rico. Years ago they were almost extinct due to land clearance and the use of these precious woods for beams and firewood. Today, however, the hardwoods, such as mahogany, are protected by conservation laws. Other decorative trees grow all over the island: the royal poinciana, or flame tree (*flamboyán*); the royal palm (*palma real*) and the coconut palm (*coco*); the West Indian boxwood (*roble*); the laurel and the Queen of Flowers (*Reina*

5

Breadfruit

de las Flores), with its blossoms which resemble lilacs; and the *acacia nudosa*, resembling the beautiful cherry blossoms.

Fruit-bearing trees, including the mango, the avocado, and the breadfruit (*panapén*), grow in Puerto Rico, as well as all the citrus fruits and over a dozen kinds of bananas.

The bright red *acerola,* or *cereza colorada* berry, which has more vitamin C than any other known natural food, grows in many backyards. Eat two tiny berries and you have your necessary vitamin C for the day! It is similar in size and flavor to the sour cherry. Puerto Ricans also love to eat some fruits that are unknown to most visitors: the *jobo* (hog plum), *quenepa* (genip fruit), *guayaba* (guava), and the *tamarindo* (tamarind). *Papaya,* or *lechosa,* is a delicacy for Europeans and North Americans, but it is a common fruit in Puerto Rico.

6

Top, papaya tree; right, mango tree

Pineapple field

Crops

COMMERCIAL agricultural products are not as important a part of the country's economy as the government would like them to be because of the relatively small territory and little amount of flat farming land. However, the various programs of the Department of Agriculture and the work of the Experimental Station are opening new possibilities for agriculture in Puerto Rico.

Pineapples have become very important to the island in the past years. The fragrant aroma of *piña* (PEEN-yah) lingers for miles on the northern coast where the fields of pineapples grow along both sides of the highways. Most of the fruit is canned, as juice or slices and pieces, right on the spot, in modern factories.

Sugar cane plantation

Cane sugar is still Puerto Rico's most important export crop. During the *zafra* (SAH-frah), or cane-cutting season, which begins in late January, the heavily laden trucks carrying the cane to the sugar *centrales*, or mills, are a familiar sight. When the cane is in "flower," it is most beautiful. The tall, graceful pink plumes bow and curtsy as they catch each breeze of the trade winds.

Driving into the foothills you see weatherbeaten, unpainted barnlike structures. These are tobacco-drying sheds and the gateway to the tobacco-growing area. Small companies manufacture cigars using pure native tobacco, but there are also large factories in Puerto Rico which

9

Fruit of the coffee tree is a "cherry." Seeds are the "coffee beans." Cherry is light green at first; turns deep crimson when ready for picking.

manufacture many well-known United States brands. They mix their local tobacco with that imported from the States and elsewhere.

Coffee is grown mainly along steep mountainsides at relatively high altitudes in the central western section of the island. Puerto Rican coffee is delicious but there is not enough of it to export in quantity. The hurricanes of the 1930's destroyed most of the coffee trees. Even more than in the continental United States, those were depression years in Puerto Rico, and many coffee growers were completely wiped out. Since it takes a coffee bush seven years to produce, almost every coffee plantation had to begin planting a faster-growing product in order to keep the family eating, or go out of business. In order to help the coffee farmer recover from hurricane damage, the government now provides insurance on the crop. Despite its small quantity, Puerto Rican coffee is among the best in the world. However, if you want to enjoy a good cup of it, you will have to go to Puerto Rico to drink it!

Birds and Animals

THE BIRDS OF Puerto Rico range from the black and yellow *reinita* (little queen), or bananaquit, who fearlessly flies into the kitchen to "borrow" a few grains of sugar, to the chattering but shy *periquito* (small parrot), who hides out in the Luquillo Rain Forest. There is also the *carpintero* (woodpecker), the *zumbador,* or *colibrí* (mango humming-bird), *rolitas* (small doves always traveling in pairs), and many other land and sea birds.

With the exception of the bat, there are no land mammals native to the island. The early colonizers told stories about a mammal rodent, a sort of big rat which the Indians ate. But this animal is long extinct.

Puerto Rico has a large share of harmless lizards, one type of non-poisonous snake, many toads, and land crabs. The land crab (*jueyes,* pronounced WHAY-ess) is ugly but delicious. Some families have a "jueyes corral" in the patio where the land crabs spend their "getting-ready-for-the-pot" period by being cleaned and fattened on cornmeal and fresh water for three weeks.

Puerto Ricans love river shrimp. These freshwater animals are sweeter tasting than their ocean-living relatives. While driving along a road near a river, you will probably see young boys selling strings of shrimp — but you can be sure that some of the catch went home to mother first!

The most fascinating of all animals in Puerto Rico is a sort of tree frog, the *coquí* (ko-KEE). This little animal sings his unique song all night long in every corner of the island. The coquí is native to Puerto Rico and not found on any of the neighboring islands. Once you have heard his happy song, "co-quí, co-quí," you will never forget him or the island of Borinquén, the Indian name for Puerto Rico.

The Waters

THE WATERS around Puerto Rico are too deep and warm to make commercial fishing very profitable on a large scale. Fortunately, this does not affect the sport fisherman. Giant blue marlin have been caught less than

11

Fishing with net

five miles from San Juan and championship records are broken time and time again.

Small-boat fishermen catch enough *pargo* (red snapper), *mero* (grouper), and *sierra* (kingfish) to take care of some of the islanders' needs, but millions of dollars' worth of frozen and dried fish must be imported annually. Among the biggest imports is *bacalao* (dried codfish), which is shipped to Puerto Rico from Newfoundland.

Small fishing village

Puerto Rico's many public beaches are a delight to all swimmers. Luquillo Beach in the northeast, ringed by swaying coconut palms, is a picture-postcard setting. It is a favorite spot for families because of its usually calm waters. To the northwest, not far from the city of Manatí, is the *Playa de Mar Chiquita*. Here the Atlantic crashes through offshore rocks, throwing the spray high into the air. Unless you are a very strong swimmer, you had better keep your distance and just watch the spectacular display.

In the south, Guayanilla Beach with its magnificent submarine gardens is a favorite spot on the Caribbean shore. La Parguera, farther to the west, is another favorite for boating and fishing, although it is better known for its unbelievable Phosphorescent Bay.

Snorkel and scuba divers head for the islands of Vieques and Culebra, or the smaller islets off the eastern coast. Here the crystal waters are home to almost endless varieties of tropical sea life.

Swimmers who are reasonably careful will never meet sharks, barracudas, manta rays, or vicious moray eels, but they do live in the waters around Puerto Rico.

A much more pleasant creature is the porpoise, or dolphin. Schools of these happy, intelligent animals can often be seen frolicking offshore.

13

Dos Bocas Dam

The manatee, or sea cow, the mermaid of imaginative sailors, lives in Puerto Rican waters. Unfortunately, fewer are seen each year as modern life pushes nature into the background.

Many streams and rivers water the island. Dams have been constructed on some of them to provide for hydroelectric power and for potable, industrial, and irrigation water. The lakes formed by the dams are favorite fishing and boating spots.

None of the rivers in Puerto Rico are wide enough or deep enough for navigation. During times of heavy rain, some of them become wild and untamable and have been known to rise ten feet in ten minutes! The longest river is the Plata, which travels forty-five miles from its source in the mountains near Cayey to the Atlantic. The Río Grande de Loíza, the Bayamón, the Manatí, the Río Grande de Arecibo, and the Guajataca are other rivers passing near the towns and sites for which they are named.

14

Mayagüez harbor

The main seaport is San Juan, but other commercial seaports in Puerto Rico are Mayagüez, Ponce, Fajardo, Guayanilla, Guánica, Aguadilla, and Jobos, near the town of Guayama.

15

International Airport, San Juan

THE COMMONWEALTH

EVERY DAY thousands of visitors arrive at International Airport, San Juan, Puerto Rico. Most of them come from the United States. They may be tourists down for a vacation, Puerto Ricans returning home, or businessmen interested in starting a manufacturing company. Many students and public officials from all parts of the world also visit the island to study the peaceful revolution that has made Puerto Rico an example of "development through democracy."

Early History

CHRISTOPHER COLUMBUS discovered the island — which he called *San Juan Bautista* — on his second voyage to the New World in 1493. The capital city was first called Puerto Rico (rich port), but in 1521 the names were switched. The capital was named San Juan and the island Puerto Rico.

Puerto Rico remained a colony of Spain for nearly four centuries, but was taken over by the United States after the Spanish-American War in 1898. The United States' flag flies side by side with the flag of Puerto

A Puerto Rican
worker

Rico, officially adopted in 1952. It has a white star on a blue triangle,
with three red and two white stripes.

The People

TODAY ABOUT two and one-half million people live in Puerto Rico. Since
they live in an area about half the size of New Jersey, this makes the
island one of the most densely populated places on earth. About one
million more Puerto Ricans live in the continental United States. They
are all citizens of the U.S. About 80 per cent of the Puerto Rican people
are of Spanish descent and the rest are a mixture of white and Negro.
Spanish is the official language, but English is widely spoken and is taught
as a second language in the schools.

Puerto Ricans are named for both their fathers and mothers. For
instance, Juan Martínez Rodríguez would be called Juan Martínez in
the United States, because Rodríguez is his mother's maiden name.

Politics and Economics

IN SPANISH, the name of the country is the *Estado Libre Asociado de Puerto Rico*. It means "Free Associated State of Puerto Rico," which is the same as Commonwealth of Puerto Rico.

During the last half of the nineteenth century, Román Baldorioty de Castro worked hard to obtain self-government from Spain. After his death, Luis Muñoz Rivera (loo-EES moon-YOH s rree-VAY-rrah) took over the struggle. In 1897, he obtained a Charter of Autonomy from Spain, which gave the island dominion status. But it was too late. The following year came the Spanish-American War and Puerto Rico passed from Spanish to U.S. sovereignty under the Treaty of Paris.

Puerto Rico's finances grew, but the people were without political and social freedoms. Until 1900, with the passage of the Foraker Act, Puerto Rico was under U.S. military rule. This act provided for a civil government, but one in which the people could only elect the members of one house in the legislature. The governor, his cabinet, and the upper house of the legislature were appointed by the President of the United States.

It was not until 1917 that Muñoz Rivera, then Resident Commissioner in Washington, obtained more self-government for Puerto Rico. This came in the form of the Jones Act, named for U.S. Congressman William Jones, who presented and sponsored the bill.

Under the Jones Act, Puerto Ricans became American citizens. They were now also given the right to elect the members of both houses of their legislature. However, the governor and other important officials continued to be appointed by the President of the United States.

The Foraker Act states that Puerto Ricans are not required to pay federal taxes because they are not represented in Congress. The act also provided that customs duties from foreign imported products were (as they still are) to be retained by Puerto Rico, and excise taxes collected on Puerto Rican products shipped to the United States were (as they are today) to be returned to the island.

Because of the tariff protection, the sugarcane industry became very

19

profitable. Within a few years the three hundred sugar mills merged into forty-two, and some of the largest were controlled by people outside the island. It wasn't long before the one-crop economy, with its seasonal employment, began to touch the lives of all Puerto Rican people. Low wages, bad living conditions, and underemployment were common all over the island.

And Puerto Rico's population explosion only added to the problem. Within thirty years, the number of people increased from 950,000 to over a million and a half!

To make things even more difficult, the island suffered two very bad hurricanes, and the great economic depression reduced Puerto Rico's exports to the United States by one-third. During the 1930's, the New Deal was extended to Puerto Rico and the U.S. government poured over 100 million dollars into the country to try to save it from disaster.

Puerto Rico's political parties developed and grew against this background. But no party was powerful enough to win an election alone. It was natural that two or more parties should join together to try to win. But they all had such different ideas about government that nothing very much could be accomplished. The result was confusion and hopelessness.

Puerto Ricans have a saying about those times. "When the stomach growls with hunger, it frightens the mind into not thinking." The politicians engaged in fruitless arguments about whether Puerto Rico should become an independent republic or a federal state. The people began to lose all interest in their government as soon as they realized that the political parties would not really work for the people's welfare.

But out of this turmoil an amazing thing happened. The Popular Democratic Party (*Partido Popular Democrático*), or PPD, was born and grew. Its leader was Luis Muñoz Marín (mah-REEN), son of Luis Muñoz Rivera. For the first time, the people were told that politics was not the primary concern of the party. Instead, the party would work for economic and social reforms.

In 1940, the young party gained control of the Senate by one seat. The balance of power in the House of Representatives was in the hands of a minority group. However, with a vote given by a political opponent,

Above, Luis Muñoz Marín at his desk; below, with the late President Kennedy.

the PPD was able to begin to carry out its promises of social justice to the Puerto Rican people.

Four years later the Popular Democratic Party won a great victory. It carried all 7 senatorial districts, 34 out of the 35 representative districts, and 73 out of the 77 townships!

The people had started to care again.

They started to care simply because a political promise had been kept. The party continued its program of reconstruction, land reform, industrialization, laws for protection of the workers, reorganization of public finances, creation of new public services, creation of public authorities for electric power, irrigation, water and sewage systems, development of agriculture, and construction of schoolrooms, roads, bridges, hospitals, and public houses.

Naturally, all this was not done in a day, and much of it still remains to be done. But once the people began to care about their own government, there could be no stopping their progress.

The Estado Libre Asociado

THEN IN 1947 the U.S. Congress recognized the right of Puerto Ricans to elect their own governor. In the election of 1948, Luis Muñoz Marín became the first elected governor in the history of Puerto Rico. He was to be elected again in 1952, 1956, and 1960.

During the pre-election campaign, the PPD promised to ask the federal Congress for a law which would allow Puerto Rico to write its own constitution and begin a new era in the relationship between the two countries.

The idea of a free associated state was not a new one, but Muñoz Marín adapted it to meet the needs of Puerto Rico.

The Puerto Rican legislature approved this plan, and in July, 1950, the U.S. Congress passed the bill as Public Law 600. The first article of the bill says, "Be it enacted by the Senate and the House of Representatives of the United States of America in Congress assembled, that fully recognizing the principle of government by consent, this Act is now adopted

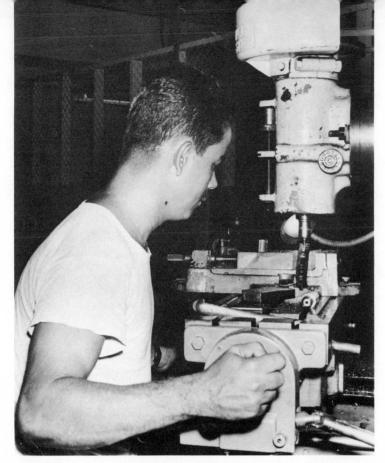

The Popular Democratic Party began a program of industrialization.

in the nature of a compact so that the people of Puerto Rico may organize a government pursuant to a constitution of their own adoption."

In 1951, 75 per cent of the Puerto Rican voters accepted Law 600, and delegates to the Constitutional Convention were elected in August of that year. All political parties were represented except the Independence Party, which decided not to propose candidates.

In March, 1952, the constitution was accepted by 375,000 voters and opposed by only 85,000. The U.S. Congress approved the constitution that year, with three amendments which did not change the essence of the document.

Jobs had to be created for many people. This is the Olympic Mill in Guaynabo.

Puerto Ricans approved the final constitution during the elections of 1952, when they gave Muñoz Marín his second term as governor. Four political parties took part in the election. The Popular Democratic Party polled 429,000 votes; the Independence Party, 126,000; the Statehood Republican Party, 85,000; and the Socialist Party, 21,000.

Puerto Rico became a commonwealth on July 25, 1952. July 25 is kept as Commonwealth Day, or Constitution Day, in Puerto Rico.

As a commonwealth, the country elects its governor and members of its Senate and House of Representatives. The governor selects his own cabinet and also names the Supreme Court justices, with the advice and consent of the Puerto Rican Senate.

The United Nations soon recognized the new status of Puerto Rico. This is a 1953 resolution as stated in the United Nations:

Considering that the agreement reached by the United States of America and the Commonwealth of Puerto Rico, in forming a political association which respects the individuality and the cultural characteristics of Puerto Rico, maintains the spiritual bonds between Puerto Rico and Latin America, and constitutes a link in continental solidarity . . . (the General Assembly) recognizes that the people of the Commonwealth of Puerto Rico, by expressing their will in a free and democratic way, have achieved a new constitutional status . . . recognizes that, in the framework of their Constitution and of the compact agreed upon with the United States of America, the people of the Commonwealth of Puerto Rico have been invested with attributes of political sovereignty which clearly identify the status of self-government attained by the Puerto Rican people as that of an autonomous political entity . . .

In the following elections of 1956 and 1960, the Popular Democratic Party obtained 433,010 and 457,880 votes, respectively; the Statehood Republican Party, 172,838 and 252,364; and the Independence Party, 86,386 and 24,103. Clearly, the new political commonwealth status was approved by the citizens.

However, it wasn't long before the minority parties started to criticize this new and unusual status of a free associated state. They are still arguing today that one congress cannot bind another and, therefore, the compact is not binding. Others say that there was no real compact to begin with because Puerto Rico was not a sovereign nation at the time of the signing. Both those who want the island to become a state and those who want independence say that Puerto Rico is a colony in disguise.

But the majority of Puerto Ricans believe that the commonwealth status, if perfected, is right for their country.

Before the November 3, 1964, election, Muñoz Marín announced that he would not run for a fifth term as governor. Mr. Marín was expected to serve on the States Commission, which was organized to look into the political destiny of the island. Roberto Sánchez Vilella, Marin's secretary of state (vice governor) for sixteen years, was elected governor. The victory meant twenty continuous years in office for the Popular Democratic Party. The PPD gained 479,479 votes; the Statehood Republican Party, 277,182; and the Independence Party, 21,885.

New homes were built.

Operation Bootstrap

IN 1940 Muñoz Marín started Puerto Rico's famous program of industrialization — "Operation Bootstrap."

One of the problems was to give people year-round work. An agricultural economy always has seasonal periods when work is slow. So the government had to find something else. Puerto Rico did not have natural resources such as oil or minerals. What the country did have in abundance were people, and so people became its great untapped natural resource!

Operation Bootstrap is not limited to promoting industry, though the Economic Development Administration (*Fomento,* pronounced fo-MAIN-to) reports almost one thousand new factories on the island. The Government Development Bank for Puerto Rico provides loans for new manufacturing industries as well as for other activities that

Industry increased.

promote the development of the economy; a fiscal agency secures financing for governmental bodies which, in turn, provide necessary facilities such as schools, roads, power, water, etc. All government departments have helped to make Operation Bootstrap a success. The Departments of Health and Agriculture had much to do before industries in the United States could be convinced that Puerto Rico was a promising place and that an alert and healthy work force would be waiting for them.

The Department of Health, working hand in hand with the Water Authority, brought water to all towns on the island, erasing most water-carried diseases. A program of sanitation, health education, and free or low-cost medicines and medical services lowered the death rate to below that in the United States. Life expectancy for Puerto Ricans in 1940 was forty-six years — now it is seventy!

The Department of Agriculture helped by aiding programs of cattle raising for fresh milk and beef, increasing chicken and egg production,

27

A Puerto Rican family stands proudly on the porch of their new home.

Hotels sprang up, such as the Americana in San Juan.

developing different crops, and distributing seeds. As a result, Puerto Ricans now eat better and are healthier.

The Department of Labor, with its special bureaus for accident prevention on the job, unemployment pay, and others, has helped management and labor to work together peacefully and well.

But the real success behind Operation Bootstrap has been, and continues to be, the willingness of the Puerto Rican people. Without their cooperation and desire, nothing could have been accomplished.

There are about 654,000 workers in Puerto Rico. About 100,000 work in manufacturing industries and 138,000 in agriculture. The rest are in commerce, transportation, public utilities, and others.

The pictures on these two pages show some of the work done by residents of rural communities in Puerto Rico to improve their living standards. The activities were carried out with the cooperation of the Dept. of Agriculture.

Operation Bootstrap helped to turn slums into lovely homes.

However, one of Puerto Rico's greatest problems is still unemployment. About 89,000 people have no regular work. As industry and health facilities developed, the population increased. At the same time, the success of Operation Bootstrap slowed down the number of people who left the country to find work in the United States. Many unskilled workers do not want to work for agricultural wages, and there is an overdemand for skilled workers. Therefore, the Department of Education, too, is very important to the success of Operation Bootstrap.

Puerto Rico still has much to do to make Operation Bootstrap a total success. But it has come far. In 1940, for example, the average yearly income was $121. Now it is $830. That is still less than half of what the average worker earns in the poorest U.S. state, but it is almost the highest wage in all of Latin America! Only Venezuela, which is rich in oil, has a higher average. And by 1970, Puerto Ricans expect to earn an average of $1,000 yearly.

After Canada and the United States, Puerto Rico ranks third in America among the countries whose income is distributed most evenly among the people. And despite its size, it is the fifth largest importer of United States products in the world and second in America — over a billion dollars a year.

The walled city of San Juan with La Fortaleza (governor's home) in fore-
ground.

1422812

SAN JUAN, THE WALLED CITY

A WONDERFUL PLACE to begin a visit to Puerto Rico is in San Juan, the capital and main seaport. Almost 600,000 people live in this lovely city on the northern coast. During rush hours, San Juan looks like any busy modern city, and the buses and cars are often stuck in traffic jams.

Most visitors want to see first the section called Old San Juan. This walled part of the city is rich in beauty and history. It is on a tiny islet just off the northeast coast, and three bridges connect it to the mainland.

You can reach Old San Juan by taking a big blue bus of the Metropolitan Autobus Authority, a public corporation. The bus stops are short yellow posts on the sidewalks that say *parada,* which means stop.

To see Old San Juan you must get off at the Plaza de Colón. Buses do not enter the narrow, century-old streets in this section. Some of the streets are still paved with the original bluish glazed blocks brought over in the old Spanish sailing ships. The parking meters are set against the buildings, and pedestrians must often walk "Indian file."

The Walls

SOON YOU ARE walking beside the walls of an old fort. This is *Castillo de San Cristóbal* (Fort St. Christopher), which was built between 1631 and 1771. It has a twenty-foot-thick fan of walls. The first shot of the Spanish-American War was fired from here.

The walls of San Juan are certainly imposing and took a great deal of time and money to build. A guide will tell you that when the King of Spain was told of the time and expense, he looked out of his palace balcony in Madrid and said in amazement, "I don't see them from here!"

El Morro

THE MOST FAMOUS of Old San Juan's forts is *El Morro,* or *Castillo de San Felipe del Morro* (Fort St. Philip on the Headland). On the grounds which surround the fort is a simple monument commemorating the removal of the Dutch general, Bowdoin Hendricks, who took the city in 1625. Hendricks asked El Morro to surrender, but the Spanish governor general, Juan de Haro, refused and the Dutch set fire to the city. However, one Spanish captain and his troops defended the castle while other troops were brought in from the main island and attacked to the rear of the Dutch. The enemy fled, and shortly afterward began the construction of the famous walls surrounding the city.

History seems alive as you cross the bridge over the old moat and walk about the ramparts of Morro Castle. The eighteen-foot-thick walls rise one hundred and forty feet straight above the water. Work began on the fort in the middle of the sixteenth century, and additions and improvements were made for the next two hundred years! When completed, it was successfully able to defend the entrance of San Juan from the attacks of the English, Dutch, and French.

The dungeons of the fort have held many prisoners, among them Francisco Miranda, the pioneer of Latin American independence. Many Puerto Rican patriots who wanted self-government were also imprisoned in El Morro, accused as enemies of Spain.

36

El Morro

Left, Christo Street; above, La Fortaleza

Historic Buildings

JUST OUTSIDE the large grounds of El Morro is the old Santo Domingo Convent, built in 1523 by Dominican friars. Today it is the administration offices of the U.S. Army.

If you walk on Cristo Street, you are standing on a once-famous raceway. Horse racing was a popular sport with *caballeros* during the nineteenth century. A story is told that one day a rider could not stop his horse when they reached the end of the street. Both horse and rider flew over the wall. Amazingly, the rider was not killed. To thank God, the rider's relatives built a chapel on the spot. However, historians say that the rider did die, and the chapel was built to prevent more racing accidents. Whichever story is true, tiny Cristo Chapel (*Capilla del Cristo*) is a shining jewel at the end of Cristo Street.

A few paces from it is *La Casa del Libro,* the House of the Book. Now a museum for rare books, it is a beautifully restored eighteenth-century building.

Not far from the chapel is the Palace of Santa Catalina, better known as *La Fortaleza.* It is the home and headquarters of the governor of Puerto Rico. The original building, destroyed by the Dutch in 1625, was a tower surrounded by walls, built to protect the city.

La Caleta de las Monjas   San Juan Gate

A short walk up Cristo Street will take you to San Juan Cathedral, where there is a marble tomb with the remains of Juan Ponce de León, founder of the Spanish colony of Puerto Rico, and also its first governor. The Cathedral faces a short and narrow street, *La Caleta de las Monjas* (Little Street of the Nuns), which leads to the San Juan Gate, also called the Water Gate because it opens the city to the sea. On a bluff nearby is *La Casa Blanca* (the White House), once the home of the Ponce de León family. It is occupied today by the commander of the U.S. Army on the island, and is part of the Fort Brooke post.

Another short walk up Cristo Street will take you to the quaint Church of San José and the plaza where there is a statue of Ponce de León made from the cannons that were captured from the British. San José is one of the oldest churches in America.

The Streets

RESIDENTIAL STREETS in Old San Juan, such as Luna, Sol, and San Sebastián, are often crowded with cafés and people. Everywhere people seem to be in excited conversation. You hear Spanish "hit tunes" on jukeboxes. You might also see men holding fighting roosters in their hands. Cockfighting is a favorite sport in Puerto Rico. Other people are discussing the tickets they bought in the weekly lottery. Lottery money is used by the government for public welfare.

The houses along the streets are Spanish colonial. A number of these old homes are being restored by the Institute of Puerto Rican Culture, which also gives technical aid to those who wish to restore their own homes. All interiors have high-ceilinged rooms and tiled floors. Most have their original ceiling beams. Made of *ausubo,* a very hard wood, they have been there over one hundred and fifty years! Many houses also have indoor patios.

Another interesting place in Old San Juan is the *Plaza de Armas,* also known as the *Plaza de Baldorioty de Castro.* On the north side of the plaza is the *Alcaldía,* or city hall. Under its Roman-style arcade, vendors sell flowers and newspapers, fruits and lottery tickets. On the west is the *Intendencia,* which houses various offices of the Commonwealth Treasury Department. This part of the city retains a colonial feeling that not even the nearby department stores and supermarkets can change.

There are many other interesting places to visit in the old section of the city. The *Tapia Theatre,* built in 1832, is used as a playhouse and for ballet. The *Ateneo,* founded in 1876 by Puerto Rico's leading poets and men of letters, is a Moorish-style building. *El Capitolio,* the capitol building, begun in 1925, looks almost out of place in the city. It is big, made of white Georgia marble, and built in the style of those in the United States. Its interior is beautifully decorated with murals depicting highlights of the history of Puerto Rico.

The southern part of the old city fronts on the bay. Here are the banking houses, the post office, insurance companies, cable and telephone buildings, the federal court, and the customshouse. It's all big business

41

Side view of capitol and new annex

Passengers debark at Old San Juan pier.

in this downtown area. The tempo is no different than in any other modern city, but it is still "miles apart" from uptown San Juan, just four blocks away.

The Dragon

FROM THIS AREA you can see a flat peninsula jutting out into the bay. It is called *La Puntilla* (the Little Point), and an exciting story is told about it.

The famous English explorer Sir Francis Drake, whom the Spaniards called "the Dragon," heard about a great treasure stored in San Juan to be shipped to Spain. On the night of November 23, 1595, Drake sailed a large fleet near the *Isla de Cabras* (Goat Island), which can also be seen from the southern part of Old San Juan. But Spanish frigates barred the entrance to the bay. Drake tried to land by sending a number of men in small boats, well-armed and with incendiary bombs. They succeeded in setting fire to all the Spanish frigates. But the Spaniards quickly put out all the fires, with the exception of that of *La Magdalena*. This ship was completely destroyed but, by the light of its fire, the Spaniards were able to inflict great losses on the English. The emptyhanded flight of Drake and his men from La Puntilla was cause for great celebration in San Juan.

43

Modern home in San Juan

Cumberland's Fall

THE BRIDGES which separate the islet of San Juan from the main island mark an historic spot. In 1598, during a second English attack, the Earl of Cumberland fell off a bridge here. He almost drowned and had to give the command to one of his officers. Still the English forces managed to capture San Juan. But after only five months, the English were conquered — not by Spaniards but by an epidemic of dysentery. Five hundred English lives were lost before Cumberland and his remaining men decided to give up their hard-won land.

The New City

THE NEWER SECTION of San Juan spreads back over the mainland, and is still growing at a rapid pace. This is mainly a residential, resort hotel, and social club area, although there are businesses here, too, and fine shopping centers. Beautiful luxury hotels ring the beaches, and it is here that many visitors stay when they visit Puerto Rico. Large, modern housing developments surround the city; new schools and factories are being

New San Juan is growing at a rapid pace.

Aerial view of the University of Puerto Rico

built regularly. The huge, modern International Airport is only fifteen minutes from the center of the city.

The University of Puerto Rico

ABOUT SEVEN MILES from San Juan, in the suburb of Río Piedras, is the University of Puerto Rico. Founded in 1903 as a one-building normal school, it has grown into a complex institution which has graduated over forty thousand students.

The university buildings and grounds are truly beautiful. Through the iron gates of the entrance, giant trees shade acres of rolling lawn. Groups of animated students are everywhere, and the girls especially seem to dress unusually well.

Twenty-one seals of the Americas, the seal of Puerto Rico, and those

On campus of the University of Puerto Rico

of many universities decorate the façade and the floor of the entrance to the main buildings.

Students graduate from the Colleges of Natural Sciences, the Humanities and Social Sciences, or of Education, Law, Business Administration, Medicine, Dentistry, and Pharmacy, as well as from the Institutes of Cooperatives, Social Work, Labor Relations, Public Administration, Social Research, and Caribbean Relations. The College of Agriculture and Mechanical Arts is located in Mayagüez on the west coast.

With a total enrollment of over twenty thousand students, including those in extension and evening courses, the University of Puerto Rico is among the ten largest U.S. land-grant colleges. The faculty numbers more than twelve hundred and the annual budget for the university is over 35 million dollars.

Education

PUERTO RICO's educational system is modeled after that of the United States, with some changes.

During Spanish occupation, education developed very slowly. By the end of the nineteenth century, there were 529 elementary schools, attended by a little more than 25,000 students from the population of 950,000. On the entire island there were only two or three schools of higher education.

When Puerto Rico came under the American flag, the public school system was set up after U.S. models. Until 1948, the Commissioner of Education was appointed by the United States President.

At first there was much confusion about the teaching *of* English and teaching *in* English. Today English is taught as a second language, and all other subjects are taught in Spanish. Puerto Rican students want to learn English, not only because of their relationship to the United States, but because of the cultural, scientific, and practical value of the language.

Many families in Puerto Rico today benefit from the Department of Education. Besides the public and private schools, the University of Puerto Rico, The Catholic University at Ponce, and the Inter-American University at San Germán, there are free adult education classes, book-mobiles, community education programs, educational television, and many other activities. In 1900, Puerto Rico's illiteracy rate was 80 per cent. Today it is 15 per cent. Nearly 80 per cent of the school-age children are in schools.

But there is still a lot to do. The island doesn't yet have enough resources to ensure that every child will have the chance to go to school. More money is needed to pay teachers well, to build classrooms, and to buy books and teaching materials.

Native Art

THERE IS not much native art in Puerto Rico, but the remains of one ancient craft survive. These are the carved wooden figures known as

Hiram Bithorn sports stadium in San Juan

santos (saints). The *santeros,* or carvers of these saints, modeled them after the religious figures that were used in Spanish churches. But the *santos* they carved are simpler and more graceful than the old devotional figures.

Sports

BESIDES SWIMMING and fishing, Puerto Ricans enjoy many other sports. There is horse racing all year round at *El Comandante* racetrack, a short distance outside of San Juan. Tennis, basketball, and boxing are popular. Cockfights are held all over the island at *galleras* (cockpits). Perhaps most popular of all is baseball, and major league stars from the States compete from October to February. Enthusiastic baseball rooters in Puerto Rico are called *fanáticos.* Many Puerto Ricans also play on the teams of the major leagues in the United States.

New buildings in the San Juan metropolitan area

OUT ON THE ISLAND

East and South

AFTER you have seen San Juan you will want to visit the rest of the island. As you leave the city in a lumbering line of trucks and buses, taxicabs and cars of all makes and sizes, it seems that all of the 740,000 inhabitants of the San Juan metropolitan area are on the move.

Santurce, Hato Rey, and Río Piedras are thriving suburbs of San Juan, which together with the nearby regions of Guaynabo, Cataño, Trujillo Alto, Carolina, and Bayamón make up the metropolitan area.

There are many factories located here, but the government would like more factories out on the island. That is why it is giving special incentives to companies that will start manufacturing operations outside the capital area.

When industry groups in one place, slums are created and the housing standards drop even though the workers earn more money. Fortunately, with the help of the federal government, Puerto Rico is getting rid of slums. Many public housing developments are being built. Every time a new one goes up, it contains more and better facilities for the tenants.

A private housing project in Río Piedras

Rents are fixed depending on the family's income. The rents are raised or lowered according to the current financial status of the tenant.

Private housing developments, or "urbanizations," are growing, too. The one-story houses with their deep lawns all show loving care. The Puerto Rican Planning Board has set up guidelines for builders. In the future, all new developments will have cultural centers, children's playgrounds, and landscaped walkways. Telephones and electric lines will be underground, and within walking distance of every house will be shops, a school, a church, etc.

Modern 4-lane highway

Most Puerto Ricans dream of owning their own homes. This dream is coming true for many, as thousands of houses, in all price ranges, are being built every year, and there is no sign of a slowdown.

Modern highways, bounded on both sides by colorful trees or graceful bamboo stands, lead away from the capital. To the east along the coastal plain are towns with picturesque names, such as Canóvanas, Loíza Aldea, Río Grande, and Ceiba.

Industry in Guaynabo

The lands around the Loíza Aldea region, which originally belonged to the Loaíza family, relatives of Ponce de León, are very fertile, and are bathed by the Río Grande de Loíza. In early times the Spaniards imported African slaves to work on them. Today most of the citizens in this area are descendants of these slaves.

The first Negro slaves were brought from Spain at the beginning of the sixteenth century. In 1817 their importation from Africa was prohibited, and in 1873 slavery was abolished.

The town of Loíza Aldea has an interesting *fiesta* on St. James Day, the patron saint of the town. St. James, or *Santiago,* is also the patron saint of Spain. On this occasion people wear grotesque masks, and there is a mock battle between the Christians and the Moors. Special masses are said; there are parades and dancing in the streets.

Puerto Ricans have many traditional fiestas of their own, though they also celebrate the main United States holidays. Among their special religious days, for instance, is the Three Kings' Day, or Epiphany, on January 6. Under their beds, children place boxes filled with grass for the camels of the Three Kings. In return, presents are left for them. Children also receive presents on their birthdays and on their saints' name days. Commonwealth Day is celebrated on July 25 and Discovery Day on November 19.

To the east is the beautiful Luquillo Range and Luquillo Beach. To the south of the town of Luquillo, *El Yunque* (el YOON-kay), which means "the anvil," 3,483 feet high, stands guard. On the side of this mountain is the National Rain Forest, a public recreation area in which there are a natural freshwater pool, a picnic area, a restaurant, and overnight cabins. Puerto Ricans, as well as tourists, enjoy the giant tree ferns and other plants of the tropical rain forest.

Young people enjoy the dense, tropical beauty of Puerto Rico's Rain Forest at El Yunque.

Fajardo harbor

Farther to the east is the town of Fajardo (fa-HAR-doh), a sugarcane center and port. From here you can take boats to the islands of Vieques and Culebra. These two Puerto Rican islands are very lovely, but their populations have decreased greatly in the past years, mainly because the U.S. Navy and Marines have taken over so much of the land.

Farther down the east coast is Roosevelt Roads, a giant United States naval base, located between Fajardo and Naguabo. Inland is fruit, tobacco, and cane country. Small rivers water the area, great rocks dot the hillsides, and flowers bloom beside every house. Throughout the countryside, in towns such as Humacao, Yabucoa, and Juncos, the smoke-blackened chimneys of sugar centrales smudge the bright blue sky.

In the east central part of the island is the city of Caguas (KAH-gwahs), the birthplace of Puerto Rico's foremost romantic poet, José Gautier Benítez (ho-SAY goh-tee-AH bay-NEE-tess). Public and private housing developments surround the city and there is also a large, modern cigar factory.

On the way to Cayey (kie-YAY) in southeastern Puerto Rico, the road curves between high hills where farmers plow with teams of oxen at unbelievably steep angles. Suddenly, in the valley, is the city of Cayey, a large tobacco center.

In the nearby mountain towns of Aibonito, Barranquitas, Comerío, Cidra, and Aguas Buenas lives the *jíbaro* (HEE-bah-ro), independent and unique among Puerto Rican people.

Top, Caguas highway;
bottom, Barranquitas

Historians tell us that the ancestors of the jíbaros were in large part stowaways and deserters from the Spanish merchant marine and armies. They knew little of agriculture, but the fruits and vegetables and fresh river fish in the area provided them with food. When the Spanish put a trade monopoly on Puerto Rico, the jíbaros restored to smuggling.

No one knows how the jíbaros could tell when small boats from the French, Dutch, or English islands were due, but on certain moonless nights they would leave the safety of the mountains and steal down to the beaches. They exchanged local goods, such as leather, cattle, fruits, and tobacco, for cloth and agricultural tools.

Then for many years the jíbaros lived simply, isolated from their fellow citizens. Most of them were poor and illiterate. However, life for the jíbaros began to change with the beginning of the twentieth century. Modern transportation and communications helped to bring about this change. Today they are integrated into Puerto Rican life. Many of their children study at the University of Puerto Rico; others work in industry or agriculture.

However, the jíbaros still remain strongly independent, but are very cooperative with one another. They have built self-help houses, schools, and even small bridges, working with the Community Education Division of the Department of Education.

On the southern Caribbean coast are the towns of Guayama (birthplace of Luis Palés Matos, one of the great poets of Hispanic America) and Salinas. You can sample delicious Puerto Rican food in restaurants that overlook the sea. The menu might include a dish of rice and red beans, nicknamed *matrimonio* (married couple) because they go so well together; *lechón asado* (roast pork); *asopao de pollo* (a soupy, rich chicken dish); boiled green bananas; *serenata* (a codfish dish); *pasteles* (a variety of chopped meat and rice, or other mixture, wrapped in plantain leaves), and *tostones* (salted, fried plantain chips). A wonderful dessert is *bien-me-sabe,* a sponge cake covered with a sauce of coconut milk and egg yolk, or *flan,* a tasty caramel custard.

The highway to Ponce (POHN-say), Puerto Rico's second largest city, plays hide-and-seek with the Caribbean. Known as the "Pearl of the

Famous   Ponce   fire house

South," Ponce, with 155,000 people, has a much more restful atmosphere
than San Juan. Although the city is building up its industry, it retains its
Spanish flavor and distinctive architecture.

In the center of the city is a large double plaza which surrounds the
Cathedral of Our Lady of Guadalupe. The city hall stands at one end
of the plaza and along another side is the old firehouse (*Parque de
Bombas*). Said to be the most photographed building in Puerto Rico,
this garish old structure is a "coat of many colors."

59

Ponce is home to The Catholic University (nearly four thousand students), the Museum of Fine Arts, and a beautiful modern hotel perched on a hill overlooking the city. Manuel G. Tavárez and Juan Morell Campos, most famous composers of the Puerto Rican *danzas* (DAHN-sahs), or dances, were from Ponce. Puerto Rico's national anthem, *La Borinqueña,* is a danza.

Another native music form is the *plena* (PLAY-nah), which probably originated in Ponce. The *plena* is a musical mixture of Spanish and Afro-Antillean rhythms. Each song tells a story — perhaps about a hurricane, the winning of a boxing championship, or perhaps a love story. Some are funny, some are sad. There are also beautiful modern songs by Rafael Hernández, some well known throughout Hispanic America.

In 1956, the world-famous Spanish cellist Pablo Casals came to live in San Juan and has stimulated great interest in classical music in Puerto Rico, through the holding of the Festival Casals.

In 1887, Ponce was the site of the first Autonomy Assembly presided over by Román Baldorioty de Castro. It was here also that Luis Muñoz Rivera founded his first newspaper.

About twenty minutes' drive to the west of Ponce, on the way to the town of Guayanilla (gweye-ah-NEE-yah), there is a complex of oil refineries, evidence of the south's industrial growth.

Across the Yauco River is the town of Yauco (YOW-koh), made famous in the nineteenth century by coffee. Many former coffee plantation workers have deserted the industry for better pay in the States or in the island's new factories. Though the coffee industry is being revived through government programs, it will probably never again be an export crop.

South of Yauco is Guánica (GWAH-nee-kah), where American troops landed in 1898. The bay is small but deep and very beautiful with its bottleneck entrance. To the east of it are lovely beaches, and to the west is the small seaside resort of La Parguera. From here boats leave nightly for the Phosphorescent Bay.

The Phosphorescent Bay is a truly marvelous natural phenomenon. A slight disturbance of its waters will set up glistening circles or shooting shafts of light which hardly fade away before others catch fire. You might think that you are looking at an inverted sky during a riot of "falling stars." This is all due to tiny, luminous organisms, highly concentrated in these waters.

The southwest corner of Puerto Rico, Cabo Rojo, is known as *La Esquina Caliente,* "the hot corner." The name comes not from the climate, as you might think, but from the character of its people. Ramón Emeterio Betances, patriot and great abolitionist, was born here. This was also the home of a noted pirate, Roberto Cofresí.

But the most famous corsair (a pirate who had the approval of his government) was Miguel Henríquez. King Philip V of Spain once presented Henríquez, a former shoemaker, with a medal and proclaimed him "Captain of the Sea and of War" because of his loyalty to the crown.

Today "the hot corner" is an important center of the salt industry.

To the west and slightly north, off the coast, is Mona Island, separated from Puerto Rico by Mona Passage, once home to Indians and later a lookout for pirates. Today only wild pigs, goats, iguanas, and three government weather observers live there.

West and North

ONE OF THE oldest settlements in Puerto Rico is in the west at San Germán (sahn hair-MAHN). The city was first built on another location along the coast. However, it was destroyed so many times by Indians and pirates that the entire population moved to its present site in 1570. The famous poetess and patriot, Lola Rodríguez de Tío,was born here in the nineteenth century. San Germán is also the home of the Inter-American University with over 5,000 students.

A climb of twenty-four steps to the Gate of Heaven (*Porta Coeli,* pronounced POHR-tah CHE-lee) will take you to the cool, old chapel built in 1606. The Institute of Puerto Rican Culture has restored Porta Coeli and it is now a museum of religious art.

Just south of the city is the Lajas Valley. Dry but fertile due to irrigation, this area is becoming increasingly productive.

Left, Porta Coeli; below, cattle grazing

Cattle is a growing island industry, too. As you pass herds of them, you also see white egrets. These birds, seen in Puerto Rico only since 1950, live with every herd, perching on the heads or backs of the animals or calmly walking between their feet! When the cattle stir up the insects in the ground, the birds are able to eat without working for their meals.

Puerto Rico's third largest city (87,000 people) is Mayagüez (mah-yah-GWA-ce), about half an hour's ride to the northwest of San Germán. The University of Puerto Rico's College of Agriculture and Mechanical Arts is located here, as well as the Federal Agricultural Experimental Station. Mayagüez is making rapid steps toward modern living — everywhere are new roads, new public and private housing developments, and modern factories. At present, the dock area is being modernized, for Mayagüez is an important port. The city is also the birthplace of Eugenio María de Hostos, writer, sociologist, and teacher, well known and loved throughout the Antilles and South America.

To the north is the town of Añasco, where Indians conducted their first "experiment" on the Spaniards, whom they considered gods from across the waters.

Early in the sixteenth century, Captain Diego Salcedo was in the area of Añasco. His Indian guides were taking him to a gold mine. When they came to a river, the guides offered to carry Salcedo across so he would not get wet. Once in the center of the river, the Indians dropped the captain and "accidentally" held him under water. Then they picked him up and rushed him to the bank, saying, "Don't be angry because we tripped and you fell in the water. It was an accident, we swear it!"

Naturally, the captain drowned. But at first the Indians didn't believe that he was dead. They thought he was just pretending. When they discovered that he had really drowned — proving that the Spanish were as mortal as the Indians — many battles began.

Farther north is Aguada (ah-GWAH-dah). The citizens of this town have put up a monument which says that Christopher Columbus landed there. However, the town of Aguadilla and other places on the western

63

Coast near Arecibo

coast also claim that Columbus landed there. Aguadilla has a hotel located on a hill, and from there you can see the town spread out below, with its docks where the sugar boats load.

The view from many points along the Atlantic coast is very beautiful, as the cliffs come right down to the sea. In one place you can see a small tunnel at the edge of the water. Until a few years ago, a narrow gauge railroad traveled around the island and passed through the tunnel. Now the train is gone but the tunnel is a reminder of a more leisurely life.

This is sugarcane and pineapple country, and it is also the land of cattle.

On the northern coast is Arecibo (ah-rray-SEE-boh), one of the oldest cities in Puerto Rico, founded in 1556. A plaza is built on the site of a small fort where Lieutenant Antonio de los Reyes Correa turned back an English attack in 1702. For this, the king promoted him to captain and gave him a gold medal. Not far from the city is a deep cave with Indian drawings carved on the stone.

Sugarcane is grown in this area, too, and a sugar central, Cambalache, is located here. The central belongs to the Land Authority of Puerto Rico, and some of the cane fields are Proportional Profit Farms. In 1900, the U.S. Congress passed a law which said that corporations in Puerto Rico could not hold more than five hundred acres of land. But the law was not enforced, and before long the best land was owned or controlled by a few corporations. In 1941, however, after the Popular Democratic Party came into power, the five-hundred-acre law was revived and enforced. The Land Authority was created to purchase the excess acres from the corporations. The land was then divided into farms. Since the start of the Proportional Profit Farms, millions of dollars' worth of profits have been shared by the workers.

There are many interesting places to visit in the mountain area to the

Proportional Profit Farm

Caonillas Dam near Utuado

south of Arecibo. In Lares, a short-lived but serious attempt to obtain independence for Puerto Rico took place in 1868. Utuado is near two large dams that supply some of Puerto Rico's electricity. Adjuntas borders one of the forest reserves. Jayuya is the birthplace of Puerto Rico's great humorist, Nemesio Canales. Farther south is the town of Villalba, and nearby the village of Collores, birthplace of Luis Lloréns Torres, a great, popular poet. Both towns are within the Caribbean National Forest, a public recreation area and forest reserve. Close by is La Punta, 4,389 feet high, the island's tallest mountain.

In north central Puerto Rico is the city of Manatí, surrounded by sugarcane lands. The name may have come from the fact that so many manatees used to live in the surrounding waters.

Puerto Rican people tell an old legend about a manatee. Centuries ago, an Indian chief and a manatee became friends. Every day the Indian would visit the lagoon where the manatee lived and call out to him. Each time, the manatee would come in answer to the call. When the Indian died, the manatee (crying human-type tears, so they say) also died. The legend says that the animal died of a broken heart.

66

Golf course at Dorado

The trip from Manatí back to San Juan is one of new factory buildings, housing developments, tiny shacks, flowering trees, and seven-foot-tall poinsettia (*flor de Pascua*) blooms. You bypass small towns with names such as Vega Baja, Vega Alta, and, close to the Río de la Plata, the town of Dorado.

Dorado is becoming Puerto Rico's most famous luxury resort area. Magnificent new hotels, velvety golf courses, and proud palms border the beautiful crescent coves. The city is only about ten miles from San Juan.

A short distance away is the fastest growing city in Puerto Rico, Bayamón. In less than ten years, thousands of new homes, two giant shopping centers, and great clusters of industrial developments have been built.

Just across the bay from the capital is the town of Cataño. Regular ferry service connects it with San Juan. Fort Buchanan, a large Army base, is on the outskirts of the town. Close by is the site of Caparra, where Ponce de León built a fortress-house. Only the foundations remain, but it may be rebuilt from descriptions which were left by Ponce de León.

PUERTO RICO TOMORROW

PUERTO RICANS everywhere are interested in politics and current events. They look forward to a better life for themselves and for their children. And they are concerned about the future of their country. What changes will tomorrow bring?

Some Puerto Ricans want their island to become the fifty-first State of the Union. Others think that Puerto Rico should be an independent country. But the greatest number of people, as the elections have shown, want to continue their commonwealth status. They want to keep their relationship with the United States and still retain their own national culture. They feel strongly that there must continue to be goodwill and understanding between them and their fellow citizens on the mainland.

However, many Puerto Ricans also feel that their commonwealth status must be clarified. The relationship of Puerto Rico with the United States should be redefined. These changes would not alter the basic elements of the association but they would give Puerto Ricans more authority to deal with their own affairs.

These are the reasons why many Puerto Ricans are so interested in politics and current events. They are making history and they know it.

68

SOME PUERTO RICAN WORDS

Acerola (ah-say-ROH-lah), or *cereza colorada* (say-RAY-sah ko-lo-RAH-dah) — A bright red fruit similar in size and flavor to the sour cherry found in the continental United States.

Adiós (ah-DYOHSS) — Goodbye.

Arroz con pollo (ah-ROS kohn POHL-yo) — Rice with chicken; a common dish in Puerto Rico.

Asopao (ah-SOH-pow) — A thick rice soup with native herbs, asparagus tips, and peppers. It is often used to accompany a meat dish.

Bandera espanola (bahn-DAY-rah ess-pahn-YOH-lah) — A canna lily which actually resembles the Spanish flag.

Buenos días (BWAY-nohs DEE-ahss) — Good day.

Carpintero (car-pin-TAY-ro) — The Puerto Rican woodpecker which is common in the interior, especially in the coffee country.

Coco (KO-ko) — The coconut palm, which is plentiful in Puerto Rico and especially picturesque along the beaches. *Coco* also refers to the coconut itself. Popular at roadside stands, one may buy it — *coco frío* — chilled and pierced so that one may drink the milk through a straw.

Coquí (ko-KEE) — A tiny, singing kind of tree frog which comes in a wide variety of colors from dark brown to pale clay.

Danza (DAHN-sah) — A romantic and sentimental musical composition which was originated in the nineteenth century.

Fiesta (fee-ESS-tah) — Festival, celebration.

Flamboyán (flahm-boy-AHN) — The royal poinciana, or flame tree, one of the most publicized of the island's trees. It is especially beautiful in summer when it is covered with bright red blossoms.

Gracías (grah-SEE-ahss) — Thank you.

Guayaba (gwah-YAH-bah) — The fruit of the guava tree. It can be eaten raw, but it is generally used for jams, jellies, sherbets, and drinks.

Jíbaro (HEE-bah-ro) — A small farmer, rural worker, or laborer. The *pava* (PAH-vah), or straw hat, is widely worn by the *jíbaros*.

Jueyes (WHAY-ess) — Land crabs are a local delicacy and are served in all restaurants.

Lechón asado (lay-CHOHN ah-SAH-do) — Barbecued pig is traditional for such celebrations as Christmas. The pig is seasoned and a pole is stuck lengthwise through it. Then it is roasted over an outdoor fire. It is usually served with a hot pepper and garlic sauce called *ajilimojili* (ah-hee-lee-MOH-hee-lee).

Muy bien (mwee byen) — Very well.

Palma real (PAHL-mah RAY-ahl) — Spanish name for the royal palm, which grows all over the island. It is the heart cut from the top of these palms that is used for the expensive heart-of-palm salad.

Panapén (pah-nah-PANE) — Breadfruit, a fruit about the size of a cantaloupe. *Tortitas de panapén* (toor-TEE-tahs) are breadfruit fritters.

Piña (PEEN-yah) — Pineapple; large fields of this fruit are found in the coastal plains west of Manatí.

Plátano (PLAH-tah-no) — Plantain, a variety of banana which is never eaten uncooked — it is usually baked, fried, or boiled.

Plena (PLAY-nah) — A folksong which combines a lively African rhythm with a Spanish melody.

Por favor (por fah-VOHR) — Please.

Reinita (ray-NEE-tah) — The most abundant bird in Puerto Rico, the *reinita,* or banana quit, is four inches long, with a yellow breast, dark upper surface, and white eyebrows. Fond of sugar, it will often fly in open windows and pick crumbs off the table. Some people leave bowls of sugar on the windowsills just to feed the *reinitas.*

Sí (SEE) — Yes.

Tamarindo (tah-mah-REEN-do) — Tamarind; small pink and white flowers dot this tree when in bloom. The sweet-sour pulp contained in the seed is used to make chutney and soft drinks.

Tostones (tohss-TONE-ays) — Slices of plaintain which have been fried, flattened, and fried again.

Zumbador (sum-bah-DOOR), or colibrí (ko-lee-BREE) — A mango, or golden, hummingbird, characterized by a golden sheen on its green-black wings and back and a yellow breast.

INDEX